Romana ... acios

by Linda Brandon
illustrated by Keri Lee Stevens

 HOUGHTON MIFFLIN BOSTON

Romana Acosta Bañuelos does important work that she enjoys. She is a banker and a business owner. Also, she was treasurer of the United States for three years. Here is a story about how she got to do these jobs.

Romana was born in Arizona. Then her family moved. She grew up in a mining town in Mexico. In 1944 Romana moved to Los Angeles, California.

Romana was a hard worker. She ran a tortilla stand. Tortillas are flatbreads made from corn flour. Romana's tortillas were very good. Her business grew.

Soon Romana opened a big food business. The company is called Ramona's Mexican Food Products. It became one of the largest Mexican food businesses in the United States.

In 1964 Romana opened a bank. In many banks at that time, workers spoke only English. The workers at her bank spoke English and Spanish. Her bank has helped many people who speak Spanish. They can save and borrow money there.

In 1971 President Richard Nixon chose Romana to be treasurer of the United States. She took care of money for the government. She was the first Mexican American woman to have that job.

Romana helps many other Mexican Americans. She gives money to students for college. This helps them get the jobs they want, just like Romana did.